Getting Calls

How to Increase Your Market Share with Your Funeral Home Website

By Robin Heppell

Copyright © 2014 Robin Heppell
All rights reserved.
ISBN-10: 150326405X
ISBN-13: 978-1503264052

Here's What's Inside...

4   Introduction

5   Getting Calls!

5   Why Don't More Funeral Home Websites Bring in Calls?

6   Don't Focus on the Technology, Focus on Marketing...

10   Why Your Website Is Your Number One Marketing Asset...

12   The Five Things Websites Need to Bring in More Calls...

21   Why Obituaries and Condolences Hold the Key to Future Calls...

26   How to Benchmark Your Funeral Home Website...

29   Why Being Ranked Number One in Google Can Increase Market Share...

30   How to Avoid the Dangers of Using Proprietary Website Systems...

33   Why a Free Website Is Never Free...

40   Here's How to Increase Your Market Share with Your Funeral Home Website...

Introduction

Getting Calls!

Victoria, BC
December 2014

One of the things people often ask me is how can their funeral home website get more calls for them. We know the effectiveness of your website could be the difference between an extra 5 - 10 funerals a year depending on the size of your market.

Getting your website ranked high on Google is more science than art. There are proven strategies that work which I've been sharing with my clients for years.

I was recently interviewed where I share the difference between a so-so funeral home website and one that gets you calls. It's not rocket science, but there needs to be solid marketing strategies behind your website to get the ranking you want.

Enjoy the Book!

I hope this book educates you and helps change your way of thinking about your funeral home website and encourages you to look beyond the glitz and get a website that gets you calls.

To Your Success!

Robin Heppell

Getting Calls!

Susan: Good morning! This is Susan Austin, and I'm super excited to be here with Rob Heppell. Rob is going to be sharing with us his thoughts and ideas on how you can increase your market share using your funeral home website. Welcome, Rob.

Rob: Welcome Susan. Glad to be here also!

Why Don't More Funeral Home Websites Bring in Calls?

Susan: Why do you suppose more funeral home websites don't bring in calls?

Rob: The people at funeral homes are not marketing experts as a rule. Their specialty is in helping and working with grieving families. As a result they outsource their website development to web developers, but the web development companies don't fully understand the funeral industry. They don't understand the thought process and the decision making process that are going through the mind of a grieving family. As a result, they design a website that isn't geared for getting the best response from a family member who is grieving. A lot of the sites are developed as a result of what's more important to the developer.

Don't Focus on the Technology, Focus on Marketing...

Rob: The funeral home owners or manager or whoever is slated to take the website on are more service oriented people and don't have a lot of technological background. Their experience comes from checking out other funeral home websites. The funeral home doesn't really understand what they need or what will actually make them get more client calls because a lot of the website development marketing messages out there focus more on the technology. This introduces what I call the next technological trinket or doodad that's added to a website which doesn't have proven results and doesn't turn into new business for the funeral home, but it makes them feel like they are keeping up.

A lot of the web development companies don't fully understand the funeral process itself, and a lot of the companies who work inside the funeral industry don't understand marketing. They're technology companies offering a marketing solution. Sometimes they're focusing on the technology rather than really understanding what the client needs. That's not going to win more calls.

Susan: Do most funeral homes have marketing teams or marketing departments?

Rob: No, they usually rely upon the owner or the manager of the funeral home who more than likely has been in the business for a long period of time, and in many cases, the family has been involved for multiple generations. There is not a lot of formal or intensive experience in marketing or website technology that these funeral professionals get exposed to.

Susan: Right and back in the day a lot a funeral homes success was a result of how big their ad was in the Yellow Pages, whereas the internet has come along and has really changed the game. It is a whole different playing field.

Rob: Exactly and that's why it's so important to rank high in the search results such as Google because ranking high in Google is the equivalent to having the biggest Yellow Page ad 15 years ago. How can you create a website that actually compels a potential client family to choose them over their competitor? That's what we are going to be talking about today.

The unique thing about funeral service is that for them to get any business, someone has to die. Then from that point, their marketing has to be such that they get found and then at least get short listed, and hopefully, due to being found and providing helpful information on their website, they will get chosen over their competitor. The big point is if they don't win that initial call, and their competitor does, they've lost that call forever. That's one large piece of revenue for them, and it's just made their competitor that much stronger.

Unlike, other industries where people can choose multiple companies, whether it's painting your house or putting on a new roof, that you're going to do multiple times or you could actually get them redone if it doesn't work, with the funeral there is only one chance to serve that family, and there is only one chance to get it right. It's because there are no do-overs, and once that call is lost, it's lost forever. The funeral home has to wait until the next death and start the process again.

Susan: Yes. This isn't like going to the dentist where we may do it 2 times a year, 3 times a year. This is potentially a once-every-30 years.

Rob: Correct, and nowadays, people are not as loyal as they once were. Members of the community aren't as loyal as they were in the past. It is partly due to society in general, and partly because families are really mobile, and now a lot of families don't all live in the same community for generation after generation like in the past. Forty or 50 years ago, people were Ford families or Chevy families or Dodge families, and they always bought that type of car, after car, after car. That's the way it was. Funeral homes would say, "That family goes to that other funeral home," and that same choice is made death after death in that family. Now, there is not that same loyalty, and families are looking around for price with getting value and making sure they get value and what funeral home can serve them best at that time.

Susan: What it is about the technology that can be a little bit misleading for these funeral directors?

Rob: Some of the website development companies create flashy things to grab people's attention such as lighting of virtual candles on the website for the family. That makes people feel good, and when the funeral home owner sees that they might think, "Oh, that's really nice" because it makes them feel good and they can, in turn, think that other people have that opportunity. Where in reality, the flickering candle, whether you have them on your funeral home website or not, is not going to be the reason why one family chooses the funeral home with the flickering candles versus the one that doesn't. That draws the attention of the funeral owner when they're going through the decision making process of the new website, but in the end it doesn't result in more calls.

It certainly looks nice, and they think that it would made them look good in the eyes of the community, but at what sacrifice chasing those shiny objects are they giving up when they may not be found, or their website isn't as functional as it could be and really geared to getting that call in the decision making process.

Why Your Website Is Your Number One Marketing Asset...

Susan: Just how important is getting this right to a funeral home?

Rob: It's very important. The funeral home website is their number one marketing asset. For the amount the website costs them whether it's 3 to 5 thousand dollars or even over the course of 4, 5 years, it's costing them a couple of thousand dollars a year for maintenance and support, no other form of marketing can come close to getting them the same level of exposure. Due to the amount of traffic that's generated today from the online obituaries and people who need a funeral home, and they don't know who they're going to go to, most people turn to the web to start their search.

Their search may be part of the decision making process because they might be asking friends or asking clergy for recommendations and thoughts, but it's so easy now for people even from their mobile phone to do a quick search to see what options they have for choosing a funeral home. No other marketing tool like TV ads, radio ads, direct mail, billboards, are going to be always in the right place at the right time for when that client needs to find a funeral home fast. That website is there 24 hours a day, 7 days a week, promoting your services unlike any other form of advertising you can create. When it's done right it's a real game changer.

Let's face it; it's hard to compare funeral homes because it's the perception that the family or the client family sees when they're doing their search. If the website doesn't load fast, if it's not mobile friendly, there are a number of factors that the funeral home may not be thinking of that could easily get them crossed off the short list of someone choosing a funeral home. For example if someone is sitting with their loved one in hospice at the bed side and it's in those last days, hours, and they know that the next decision they're going to make is to choose a funeral home, they may just turn to the phone and start their search.

If they click on a funeral home website and the website doesn't load quickly, they will just go back and choose the next one on the list. That's why it's so important to make sure that those pieces of the technology, mobile responsiveness and page load speed, I believe are way more important than a flickering candle.

The Five Things Websites Need to Bring in More Calls...

Susan: Let's talk about what a successful funeral home website looks like, so their phone will ring.

Rob: There are a number of important factors for funeral home websites to get more calls. Let me reiterate again the biggest factor to help your website generate the most calls is search engine optimization, which is known as SEO, and that means get your website ranking high on Google, Yahoo, and Bing. Search engine optimization for your website needs to be built from the ground up, and not every web development company does this. Some of them offer it as an add-on service when it needs to be done right from the beginning. Google and the other search engines have made it known what they like and what they don't, and it's pretty easy to follow their instructions, but some choose to focus on other things rather than the most important one.

Susan: What kind of impact will being ranked higher make on getting calls?

Rob: From the statistics available in Google Search, the first website listed when someone does a search gets 42% of the clicks as compared to 30% for the second placed website, and it drops down from there. Search engine optimization is very important. If you aren't coming up on page 1 of someone's search, you just don't have a chance with getting their call.

Susan: Right because if they don't make the short list, it's almost like having a billboard off a back country road that no one ever goes down. It may be a great billboard, but if no one is going to see it, you're just not going to get any calls.

Rob: Correct. The second thing to get right for a successful website is once people have found your website; the funeral home needs to educate the client about why they should choose them versus another funeral home.

The 3rd thing to have for a successful funeral home website is the online obituaries and the condolences have to be done right. Every web development company provides obituaries and condolences to some degree or another, but where some fail is that they make it so that the visitor has to click through a number of different hoops to get to either the obituary or to the guest book where they can leave a condolence.

What we found is that the simpler the process for the visitor to read the obituary and in the same page be able to read and leave a condolence is best. The reason for this is first, there are more condolences, and as a grief educator, Dr. Earl Grollman stated, "Grief shared is grief diminished." The more people who leave condolences on an obituary helps the survivors know and appreciate the significance of their loved one who has passed.

If there are only 2 condolences on a guest book, it's just not going to have the same impact as 20 condolences. And so if your guest book is hard to navigate or find, it really hurts the impact of those condolences.

This also feeds back into search engine ranking. Search engines like to know that websites are being visited and while people are on the website that they're engaging with the website. The website that has 20 condolences will have a higher level of engagement than a website that has only 2 condolences for the same obituary. The search engines track that. Google gives information to people through Google Analytics, Chrome Browsers, the Google Toolbar and they're able to monitor the activity on websites. The higher interaction you have on your guest book and obituaries, it helps the Google ranking.

The 4th component for a successful funeral home website would be having the ability to create as many new pages as you want. We call these landing pages. This ensures the funeral home can communicate directly with the number of different niche markets in their community.

For example, almost all funeral homes can serve all markets because everyone is going to die eventually, but sometimes funeral homes get their marketing wrong because they try to be efficient which turns into being ineffective. When they say, "We serve all faiths." The person receiving and hearing that message isn't of all faiths. They're of one particular faith or maybe even no faith. That broad message doesn't connect with them, so the funeral home thinks they are being inclusive but really they are excluding people by default.

The ability to create individual pages which are geared just for Catholics, geared just for Jews, geared just for veterans or geared just for Freemasons, is what really allows someone to resonate with a particular funeral home. So the funeral home needs to have the ability to easily create those pages in coordination with their other marketing. They can direct the Catholics from their Catholic church bulletin, not to the home page where there is a dozen messages going on but rather they can direct them to one page that has a one-on-one conversation about how they help Catholics and that they know how to perform Catholic services.

Susan: Very good. It may be very similar to how they perform other services but here are language differences, visuals that are different, so that that individual feels like they really know they are speaking to them.

Rob: Yes, and we even have examples of companies with our websites that have gone around town and taken a photograph with them and their funeral coach outside of all of the major churches, so that they can create a page on their website for that specific church so not just the denomination. Then, when they advertise in that church bulletin at St. Patrick's Parish, people click on that link and they land on a page that has a picture of their church and with the funeral home represented there, so there is a bit of brand swapping or brand recognition of tying the 2 brands together. It will further them in the conversation in their mind of, "This funeral home understands me because they know where I worship" or, "They've been to where we're going to have the service."

Even though every other funeral could do the same, not many have that ability because they're limited to the number of pages they can have on their website, or it's just too difficult to perform that level of service.

Susan: Yes. I love that idea because it's a very stressful time when families are doing these searches, and it has to be comforting to see their church right on that page. It has to be a comfort to see that and think "Oh, I'm in the right place."

Rob: Exactly. There is a lot of psychology behind good marketing that goes way beyond, as I said earlier, flickering candles.

The 5th key factor for a successful funeral home's website ties into the decision making process of new people looking for a funeral home, by having the ability on funeral home websites to foster positive online reviews.

What I mean is, by being able to add positive online reviews to your website is looked on very favorably by clients looking for a funeral home for a loved one. No one wants to make a wrong step here, and allowing positive reviews to be posted on your website is very important. I'm not talking about fake positive reviews or anything like that. These are real testimonials from past clients.

What a funeral home can do is actually solicit reviews and build in a filtering process where the positive reviews get directed to places like Google Plus and Yelp. Negative reviews get circumvented to an online form that is then submitted directly to the funeral home. This does a couple of things. First of all, the positive reviews go to where they need to go and be out to places that Google Plus and Yelp that will help the search engine rankings, but also when people read the reviews, they can read positive ones.

By filtering the negative reviews, those negative reviews aren't ending up on those places such as Google and Yelp. Also, this way the funeral homes get notified of the negative reviews straight away, and the funeral home can address what the family is unhappy with and try to resolve the problem immediately.

This is a marketing strategy and a technology which is very beneficial to the funeral home in building a more positive and a more robust online reputation.

A bonus strategy for a successful funeral home website is, and I'll be upfront and say some funeral homes aren't always comfortable with this strategy, but this has been proven in our studies and sometimes in conjunction with using Google AdWords is having a value comparison or a cost comparison right on their website. A value comparison lists the different services that funeral home offers in a grid or matrix or table format.

Traditionally for the United States Funeral Homes - who are governed by the FTC - have to itemize all of their prices on their general price list, which makes the decision making process for the family very overwhelming. It's just paragraph after paragraph of different line items and then trying to compare different types of services within the funeral home. It's done on a very linear basis, and it's very hard to comprehend and compare.

By having a table or matrix - many other industries use this, especially online industries whether it is online data storage or maybe it is different software programs or different packages. Often you see like a gold, silver, bronze listing and you can, just by scanning the table, you can easily see the difference in the packages. People don't necessarily choose the least expensive one because they can then do a side by side comparison and actually, go, "Okay, we'll go for the next service because it's worth spending the extra thousand dollars because we see way more value in that than the lower end service offering."

Funeral homes don't have gold, silver, bronze packages, but they do have different service types from simple cremation to memorial services to celebration of life and traditional funeral. To see those all side by side, someone who is concerned about price can see that, "Okay, the lowest priced one gives me the bare necessities," and the family can choose that, if they want, but they can then see the differences between the different services offering of that one family, of that one funeral. The other strategy using the same format is to actually compare the same type of service to their competing funeral homes.

We see this a lot when buying consumer goods; if we're buying a camera or a new TV, we can do side by side comparisons and compare all the different features of what the particular products offer. The funeral home can break this down and show how they compare against their competitors and usually show that they don't have the least expensive, but they can actually be kind of in the middle or even on the higher end, but if they're providing the services they say they're going to provide, the table should show that they are a better value. It just really shortcuts and simplifies the decision making process for the client family.

We have to remember that these people are grieving and they have to make a decision that they don't want to make. If we're the ones that make it easy for them, even that alone is going to build rapport and help us get that call versus losing it to one of the competitors.

Susan: This can be very overwhelming to make these big decisions. We don't even know all the questions to ask. So I would think being able to see the comparison gives us some peace of mind that, "Oh, okay, here is exactly what I can expect." How far down the website do you put this?

Rob: This would be in under some type of service offerings section, so it's not going to be directly on the home page. 90% or even more people who are going to the funeral home website aren't interested in a price comparison. They're there to get information about someone who has died and when the service is. These cost comparisons can be created as landing pages and again, in association with things like, Google AdWords. This can be the landing page for someone who is looking to make a decision about choosing one funeral or another. In the ad, if they see the words, cost comparison, there is really good chance that they're going to click on that ad because in their mind, they know that this is going to shortcut my decision making process.

Why Obituaries and Condolences Hold the Key to Future Calls...

Susan: You mentioned earlier why websites are the #1 marketing tool for these funeral homes. What has changed to make that so?

Rob: With the benefit of the online obituaries, the funeral homes can be getting 10,000 to 50,000 visitors to their websites per month. Yet, there might really only be 10 key people they're trying to attract. Members of the community are visiting those websites because while they're living in the community, they're going to have friends or acquaintances that have passed away. The reason why the funeral home website is so important is because the newspapers obituary section is having the same fate as the Yellow Pages. In a number of major centers and even smaller communities, the number of newspaper publications is being reduced more and more every day.

Whereas before, you could wake up in the morning, go to the front door, grab your newspaper and grab your coffee and scan to the obituary column and see who died in town. If they see someone died, they could take down the funeral information and put that in their schedule. Nowadays we're only dealing with the 2 or 3 or 4 day window, maybe 7 days on the long side for when the obituary is published to when the service is going to take place. Since publishing is sometimes being reduced in a number of areas down to say 3 days a week from 7 days a week, the online obituary plays a much bigger role in the community of notifying the community of a death and an upcoming service.

If people live in the northern part of North America and they snowboard for the winter, they actually check the funeral home's website back home while they're down in Florida or Arizona or California on a regular basis and even sometimes on a daily basis. That is one way they keep in touch with the community. Other ways of keeping in touch with what's happening is that with some funeral home websites you can subscribe to their obituary feed, so that you would be notified by email if when there is a new obituary added.

One of the things online obituaries do is drive huge amounts of traffic to the funeral home website, but for most funeral home websites, when someone lands on the home page, there are a dozen or more different conversations going on. That's necessary for the bulk of the people that are going there to find service information, but it's that thin sliver of visitors that are the ones that really generate all of the revenue for the funeral homes, and those are the people who have just lost a loved one and are looking to choose a funeral home to look after those services.

Obituaries are the number one driver of website traffic to a funeral home's website because people are looking to find out information such as when the service is, where it is, or if someone has died. Since there aren't as many newspapers being published on a daily basis anymore, people still want to find out when the services are or if they've heard a rumor that someone has died. In our society today, we don't want to wait to find out tomorrow. We want to find out now. There are a number of means such as the families notifying their friends through email or through Facebook or just for the person using Google or the other search engines to find the obituary for the person who has died.

This drives the bulk of the traffic to the funeral home website. One benefit that a funeral home with online obits has over any of the other local service providers, like their friends within their rotary club or chamber or other business groups, is that marketers are always telling businesses that they need more content for their website. Content is king, and the local accountant or lawyer or estate planner is going to have to create a blog post or come up with articles to build up that foot print of their website. Funeral homes don't have to do that because their content is in the form of obituaries that need to be posted and published.

Funeral homes don't have a problem with content production as it comes in the form of the obituary. The more people that visit a funeral home website, while they're there, they are inside the virtual walls of that funeral home. That is another way that they can continually keep their brand out there without having to pay any money on brand advertising.

Susan: You're saying the funeral homes can use the obituaries to help meet that need for content?

Rob: Exactly, It's a double win for the funeral home. They are providing the service for the family by getting the funeral information published somewhere and out to the community as fast as possible, and at the same time they're getting the benefit of that because it's another page that can be indexed in the search engines.

By getting more people engaging with the obituary, reading it and leaving a condolence, and as I mentioned before, Dr. Earl Grollman stated, "Grief shared is grief diminished," the more condolences that are left for us on an obituary are first going to help the family in their grieving process. They're going to show the life of their loved ones had a lot of significance with all those people leaving those nice comments. The funeral home is a benefactor of providing that additional service to the family. They also benefit by having not just more traffic but more engagement on their website and the search engines love that, too. The funeral home really wins by making sure that their obituary program is as powerful as possible.

Susan: Do you recommend that be on the home page?

Rob: Yes, there should be a listing of the most recent obituaries on the home page, depending on the size of the firm. Maybe you only have room for the names of the people and, or maybe you have room for a little exert of the obituary and even a little thumbnail image of the person. The reason why you'd want the most recent obituaries listed on the home page would be first because people want to find out information. Those people who are snow birding or checking them instead of checking the newspaper every morning, they check the funeral home website every morning. They can just got to the home page and read that one little section or that one section of the funeral home homepage to see what new obituaries are there.

The second benefit is that the search engines, when they're crawling websites, the first page that they crawl is the home page and in their library or their index of that website, they know all the previous content, and if they find that there is something new on there, such as a couple of new obituaries, that's a key to them that this site is current, and they will then continue to crawl that website. With a lot of these strategies there is a double benefit. There is a benefit to the family and the community, and then there is also a benefit to the search engine optimization for that funeral home website.

Susan: Agreed, I don't think they should have to click 10 times to find the obituary about their friend.

How to Benchmark Your Funeral Home Website...

Susan: Can you share with us what a good benchmark for traffic is for their websites?

Rob: A funeral home might be wondering what a good benchmark is for the amount of traffic for your funeral home website. A good benchmark would be 300 to 500 visitors per call or per funeral. This doesn't mean that there is going to be 300 or 500 people attending that service, but from any other benchmark this seems to be the one that we can really regulate or really measure; the amount of exposure that the funeral home is having based on the size of their company. Some funeral homes serve 150 families a year. Other funeral homes will serve a thousand or two thousand families a year. You can't just compare website to website of traffic.

You need to base the traffic against how busy that funeral home website or how busy that funeral home is. That's why with our clients, 300 is usually kind of the minimum but most of them receive up to a thousand visits per call to their websites. Small funeral home website, serving 150 people can get in a year, so 10 to 15 in a month, could still be getting 20, 30, 50 thousands visitors per month. In one case the funeral home does such a good job with their online obituaries, the local newspaper just has a link on the newspaper's website to go to the funeral home for all the obituary listings in the community.

For the really proactive funeral home, if they want to further their marketing and harness all of this traffic, they could deploy a re-marketing campaign which is when people come to a website, there is a cookie placed on their browser. Then, as they travel around the internet, and if they land on a website, that offers ads, the funeral home ad might appear there depending on how much they bid for that. One bit of research that was done a couple of years ago by one of the insurance companies that focuses on people pre-planning and pre-paying their funerals, they surveyed their policy holders and they said that they had attended a funeral 6 months prior to making their pre-arrangements.

If we can extrapolate out of that, when they've attended the service, they have a bit of their mortality gut check and think, "Well, hey you know, if Bob died, how much longer do I have left, or maybe I should get my act in order." If that conversation is going on in the back of their head, and they've been to the funeral home website, they read the obituary, and then they go about their internet surfing, and then come across a nice branded ad which simply says, "Have you ever thought about making your own pre-arrangements or your own arrangements? Click here for a free resource." It would not be tasteful to have a pre-planning ad on the obituary on the website itself because that would be tacky. When it's done off site and on another website, then it's not going to be seen as intrusive.

Susan: Wow. That's pretty stealthy! I would imagine this could really make a key difference in that website effectiveness.

Rob: Exactly and the great thing is that the competitors can't really figure out what's going on because they're not really seeing the entire strategy and process. Even though they could employ the same process themselves.

Why Being Ranked Number One in Google Can Increase Market Share...

Susan: When someone sits down at a computer to search for a funeral home, how important is it that their website is the first, second, or third ad someone clicks on?

Rob: When we're looking at the business, we call these the up-for-grab calls. There are still people who are going to use the same funeral home they've used in the past, but there is a growing percentage of calls every month that are basically up-for-grabs. The people who have had a death in the family, and they don't already know a funeral home, and so they are actively searching. For those people who are undecided, if your funeral home website doesn't show up in the top 5, your website is not nearly as effective as it could be.

One of the reasons why it's so important to be ranked number one in Google is being ranked number one is going to get you more clicks than being ranked number two. But secondly, you want to be ranked #1 for perception. People assume Google is so smart they know something about that businesses being ranked in a certain order, so by perception alone you can be perceived as being better than all the competing funeral homes. And lastly if you have that position of being the online leader, while your competitors are obsessing over trying to dethrone you, you can be focusing on more proactive strategies to continually increase your market share.

How to Avoid the Dangers of Using Proprietary Website Systems...

One of the pitfalls that some funeral homes encounter is when they choose a website from a company who uses their own proprietary system. A proprietary system is a custom website system or content management they have built for funeral service. In the beginning it's very focused towards what funeral homes need. The problem of buying one of these websites is you really don't own your website, and because it's a proprietary system you can't pack it up and host it somewhere else. What happens is since they've built this custom piece of technology, it is solely up to them to keep that piece of technology up-to-date. When they're thinking of spending money on new research and development or thinking of spending it on profit sharing, or whatever else they're going to spend their money on, keeping up-to-date is not always their number one priority. Even though they're a technology company, they can be behind the curve in some technological advances.

Currently, not many funeral home websites offer mobile responsive websites. They either don't offer any solution at all or they offer a separate mobile version of a website. Google doesn't think that is the best way to display your content to visitors. Google recommends all websites be mobile responsive, meaning no matter what size of browser or device the website is being viewed, it adjusts to the width automatically. That's not the case of a lot of these proprietary websites.

Susan: I would imagine that with as fast as technology is progressing in this modern world, to be locked in with something out of date would be very detrimental.

Rob: If they can't adapt quickly they just feel stuck and trapped. What some website companies focus on is the sale of the website, and the transaction or the relationship really diminishes at the point that the website goes live. Where other websites which are built with the intent of being continually customized and to be able to extend their functionality, they're almost like a living organism that continually changes and adapts to its surroundings.

Another problem with the proprietary systems is they don't always have the ability to add additional pages. As we talked about previously, for creating specific pages for specific target audiences, they are usually very limiting.

Susan: You get the cookie cutter solution with only so many pages, and that's it?

Rob: Yes, and although funeral service and the process of a funeral are very similar all over North America with the process that happens, each individual business is different from whether where they're located or how many firms they have. There are a number of funeral homes that have multiple locations. Without having a lot of flexibility, you're bound or trapped in working within the confines of that proprietary system.

Probably the number one downfall is that it's more like you're leasing your website instead of actually owning it. You do not own your site when you have a system that's built on a proprietary technology, owned by the web development company, not owned by you.

Susan: Why are they attracted to these one-stop solutions is it because they don't have time?

Rob: In the beginning it was. A website was just a piece of technology, and that was an online brochure and then an online brochure with online obituaries.

Now, with the decrease in the use of the yellow pages and physical newspapers with obituaries, the funeral home website has become the main marketing hub for all of their advertising. Any type of advertising they can always then funnel them back through the website, whether it's TV or radio, print ads, they can either pick up the phone to call or they can go to the website.

The website is becoming the hub, because people can get their questions answered 24-hours a day, and death takes no holiday and has no time schedule. People are searching funeral home websites in the middle of the night or early, early in the morning. Although funeral homes have their phones answered 24-hours a day, the answering services or people that answer the phones off hours don't always have all of the information that the funeral director would have, who's on call or at the office.

Why a Free Website Is Never Free...

Susan: What about some of these so called free websites that these funeral homes sometimes probably come across. What are your thoughts on those?

Rob: Some of these free websites are for the small funeral home that's kind of in a secluded place all by themselves, without any competition, and they don't really need their website as a marketing tool. It's more as a service tool. These sites are good to get started with your online presence, but if a funeral home is in any place with competition and the need to be able to be always growing your online presence, the cost savings ends up hurting them in the long run.

The suppliers that offer these websites are not online marketers. Their main focus is their core product line, whether it is caskets or urns or vaults or chemicals. There's really not a need for them to always keep up on the latest advancements in website technology and online marketing best practices.

The other problem is, with them having access to the website, they can get some insider information from their clients. As an example, if the funeral home is using a website from a casket manufacturer, and the casket manufacturer can then see or access all the number of obituaries placed on that funeral home website over the course of a month or a year or a quarter, they could then compare that number to the number of casket sales that they've made to that company, and then wonder, hey, why do these numbers not add up? Are they getting their caskets from somewhere else? This is just as an example. Some people just don't like Big Brother watching, and that's what can happen.

The other thing with those sites is that they're designed so that their products - what's most important to them - are always very well showcased and other elements and other marketing attributes that would probably be more important for the funeral home to get more calls, take a second role on that website to the showcasing of the merchandise.

Some of the other free website schemes that are out there use the ploy of floral commissions to offset the development and the hosting of the website. The problem with this is that it is a short-sighted proposition because the increase in floral commissions would not, over the course of a year, amount to the benefits of receiving one or two extra calls from having a better-performing, higher-ranking website. Furthermore, the commission-based websites are always at a reduced commission. Where if the funeral home was to take that on themselves, they could actually experience double the commission and having a better performing website.

Just like the proprietary systems from the technology companies, the funeral home does not own their website when it comes from the suppliers. They can't move the site over. They can move the information or ask for the obituaries to be exported, and then they could go from there and build a website that they would actually own and fully control.

Susan: If a funeral home has an underperforming website, and they take your strategies to heart, and they get one which is higher ranked and has all the right features- what kind of difference have you seen this make?

Rob: There are a few differences. First, they can increase their rankings in the search engines in as short as a three-month period. Other things that they'll realize is that they end up not being as frustrated because what they've always been told that they can't do, they actually can do now. It's liberating to know that they can go in and add or change the content more easily than they could in the past. The other websites all have some form of content management system, so the user can make some changes, but the extent of the changes is greatly increased when moving to a platform that they would own, or a website that they would actually own.

Susan: Where are you from Rob?

Rob: I'm based out of the Pacific Northwest in Victoria, B. C., and I am a fourth-generation funeral director. On my Mom's side of the family, my great-grandfather started the undertaking business in Bolton, Ontario, which is just northwest of Toronto, Ontario. I was fortunate enough to grow up in Victoria, and after graduating high school, I went out to Ontario to play hockey, and while there, I lived at the family funeral home with my grandfather and my grandmother, and my aunt and uncle and my cousins lived in the house next door.

During that summer, when I wasn't playing hockey, I had to obey Grandpa's rule of, "If you can eat and sleep, you can work!" I would have to perform transfers in the middle of the night, washing the cars during the day, gardening, and spending time at the cemetery with my grandfather straightening the headstones and cutting the grass, and all those things that happen in a smaller town.

I came back to Victoria to play hockey, and my dad told me that I can't sit around all day. I was so shy, he phoned the local funeral home, McCall Brothers, and arranged an appointment for me to go down, and I talked to them. I was then hired to do similar duties there, and then shortly after that was offered an apprenticeship, and I received my funeral director's license and have been licensed for over 25 years.

One of the unique things about the market here, as in a lot of retirement markets, the competition is quite high, and the cremation rate is quite high, too, so by trial and error we had to figure out a lot of these strategies to stay in business and stay profitable. It's been like being on the bleeding edge, where we didn't have other people to ask what to do, so we had to figure a lot of it out on our own.

In 1996 I started building the McCalls website, and I have been involved in online technology ever since. In 2006, I ended up branching off on my own, creating my consultancy, Funeral Futurist, and from that time, have been able to help funeral homes throughout North America and around the world with their marketing and competitive strategies with a real focus on building their online presence.

Susan: Very good, and so the funeral homes don't have to be within driving distance of you to work with you?

Rob: No. A number of family owned funeral homes I work with are folks I haven't met face to face, but they've either read my websites or my articles in trade publications, or have seen me speak at conventions, and over time we do end up running into each other and meeting each other, and now I've got great relationships all throughout the continent.

We try to provide a level of service that, since I'm a funeral director, what the funeral home would give to their client families. We really try to provide that different level of service. The other thing, too, that we really try to focus on is when we build a funeral home website; we use a content management system that's the most popular in the world, so it's not some proprietary system. Then we give a look and a feel and a functionality that is completely customized for the individual funeral home.

Our websites can be extended to however the funeral home would want, and then based on my experience; I can let them know what are the best directions to go in, or what might be even a better angle to put on it, based on their situation. Although the process of the funerals is very similar throughout North America, every community and every situation is different depending on the makeup of the community, the number of funeral homes in the area, and just the geographical location and maybe different state or provincial regulations that they're dealing with. We can always accommodate those nuances so that they don't have to work solely within a cookie-cutter website.

When the website has been completed, the client funeral home completely owns the website. We make sure that their domain name is registered in their name. A lot of times we find that when clients transfer over to us, the domain name was not actually in their name at all; it was in the supplier's name or the web developer's name, and so we quickly change that, so it's in the client's name. During the time that we're involved, we have access to that, but they're fully in control.

One of the things that might even hurt us a little bit is that we don't have a proprietary system to lock them in. Since our sites can be basically copied and backed up, copied and moved, very easily, it means that we have to work hard every month to keep their business. But 99% of our clients, after the website is built, still have us host the website on our really stable, really fast servers, because those are the things that Google considers when ranking websites: are the sites up, and do they load quickly.

Probably the things that clients like most about the websites that we create are that they can make the changes themselves, or if they're too busy, or it's maybe a little more complicated, request that we do it for them, whatever's easiest. We're not there to nickel and dime our clients when they ask for updates. They choose their hosting package, and as they need their updates, we do it for them, and we're not charging them for every little additional request.

Here's How to Increase Your Market Share with Your Funeral Home Website...

You already know your website is integral in getting your name out there. The confusing part is not knowing how to position your funeral home website to be an industry leader.

That's where we come in. We help independent funeral homes just like yours increase your market share with your funeral home website.

Step 1: We invest 30 minutes understanding you and your market.

Step 2: We help you discover the gaps your current website is not currently employing.

Step 3: We take it from there and work with you to design a robust website which will fill those gaps and get you calls.

Most funeral directors think they need flashy websites with the latest technology gadgets to get attention.

Now you can increase your market share with your funeral home website with proven strategies implemented by an industry insider.

If you'd like us to help, just send an email to: info@GettingCalls.com and we will take it from there.

About the Author

Robin Heppell, CFSP, combines his expertise in marketing, technology, and pre-need, his formal business knowledge, and his deep-rooted legacy in the funeral profession, so that he can help funeral homes and cemeteries be more competitive, more profitable, and provide the best possible service for the families they serve.

Through his consulting firm, FuneralFuturist.com in Victoria, British Columbia, he assists funeral directors and cemeterians around the world embrace and incorporate innovative strategies, marketing plans and technologies.

This "Funeral Futurist" has over 25 years of experience in a highly competitive, high cremation (90%) market. He is a fourth generation funeral director and a Certified Celebrant. Heppell is a former faculty member of the Canadian College of Funeral Service, a contributor to Mortuary Management and the Canadian Funeral News, and his own websites include FuneralGurus.com and FuneralFuturist.com.

www.ingramcontent.com/pod-product-compliance
Lightning Source LLC
Chambersburg PA
CBHW070718180526
45167CB00004B/1521